SCHEDULE YOUR SUCCESS

To be more fruitful, accomplish more and accomplish more elevated levels of pay, you need to begin planning your prosperity. Assuming that an objective is significant enough for you to record and dream about, it's unreasonably critical to simply trust you'll carve out the opportunity to make it happen. All things being equal, you should contribute the time on a steady, regular routine to accomplish the work that will assist you with accomplishing your goals. For the greater part of us, that implies we need to plan these high need exercises into our schedule consistently. If not, different interruptions and propensities will dominate and hold us back from accomplishing what is generally vital to us.

If you don't effectively top off your day by day plan with your most elevated need and most significant work, it will naturally get topped off with less significant work. I can't stop for a minute that other stuff will be for you, however I can see you it presumably won't be the work you want to do to accomplish your most significant objectives throughout everyday life. Whenever low need exercises take up a lot of your time, you wind up feeling like you're simply too occupied to even consider making genuine progress.

When you invest the greater part of your energy finishing undertakings that you loath, or that you're bad at, or that are not guiding you where you need to go, your work and life turns into a battle to succeed. The straightforward arrangement is to plan your most significant exercises consistently and guarantee that you're taking care of your most significant responsibilities first and foremost.

Oh sure, you'd very much want to invest more energy with your loved ones, work more on your fantasy ventures and objectives, and appreciate more get-aways, however you're simply excessively occupied. Assuming that sounds like you, this book will assist you with getting your time back. It'll assist you with distinguishing the low need exercises that are sucking your time and energy and holding you back from making the progress you desire.

The initial step is to make mindfulness. Your excursion to an unheard of degree of usefulness, achievement and satisfaction is simply starting when you begin to understand the manner in which you're as of now investing your energy will not get you where you need to go.

If you need change to occur, plan it in your calendar.

STEP 1. CREATING AWARENESS BY IDENTIFYING

Unconscious Habits

The principal thing you should do to deal with your time is become mindful of your present propensities and how you really invest your experience consistently. It's significantly more straightforward to address propensities when you get them, rather than attempting to simply put fresh out of the plastic new propensities on top of all your old ones and expecting supernatural change for the time being. The world simply doesn't work that way. Generally incredible advancement occurs throughout a lengthy timeframe. We gain a little headway consistently, and that smidgen of day by day progress snowballs and makes enormous change over long stretches of time. The key is to get your snowball rolling in the right direction.

Don't worry, though. This is anything but a convoluted interaction. It doesn't require some investment. Indeed, you'll wind up accomplishing more quicker than expected and having more opportunity to appreciate life outside of work assuming that is the thing you're searching for. Gaining groundbreaking headway doesn't need to be troublesome and agonizing. Everything necessary is a little exertion and following a straightforward cycle that will make your old, unsupportive propensities become so unmistakable to you that they become simpler to change. You'll be stunned how much better you'll feel when you at last focus a light on your old, dull propensities that have been holding you back.

Most of the time, our greatest boundaries and squares to progress are the little ones in our vulnerable side. Very much like while you're driving a vehicle and there's a sure region close to or behind your vehicle that you can't see in view of your vulnerable side, in life we have vulnerable sides as well. To gain gigantic headway quick, just glance at your vulnerable sides. The issue is that we weren't shown how to do this in school. The well-known adage "obliviousness is euphoria" is nonsense!
Ignorance denies us of our wellbeing, thriving, achievement and fulfillment.

This book and this interaction you're going to learn will assist you with distinguishing your vulnerable sides and take a quantum jump toward a lot more significant level of success.

The key is to begin with your day by day propensities. What you do each day, the greater part of the day is either driving you toward your fantasies or pushing them farther away.

So what are your every day

propensities? What do you do

all day?

The entertaining thing is, the vast majority don't really have the foggiest idea what they do day in and day out. Furthermore I was one of them. That was until I begun paying attention to Jim Rohn's sound projects. In one of his projects, he shared a straightforward exercise that helped me effectively and straightaway recognize my propensities, and it changed my life.

Now I will impart it to you.

THE TIME TRACKING EXERCISE FOR IDENTIFYING YOUR HABITS

This is a one-week work out, so you will need to plan it on your schedule right now!

I exceptionally recommend you start this drawn out practice tomorrow and timetable it in your schedule at the present time. But if you're really a go-getter, you can grab a notebook and pen and start the Time Tracking Exercise exercise right now.

WHAT YOU'LL NEED:

A journal and pen with you consistently during the week.

Alternatively, you could utilize a scratch pad application in a cell phone or tablet, however by and by I incline toward an actual note pad and paper to keep away from potential interruptions from email and different warnings on my smartphone.

HERE'S WHAT TO DO:

Starting from the second you get up in the first part of the day (or at this moment for you determined workers), record what you do like clockwork. For instance, when you awaken at 7am, compose down:

7am

Then, like clockwork record the time (gauge to the closest 15 minutes) and how you helped every brief square of time during the day.

Here's an illustration of what a couple of hours in the day could look like in your notebook:

7am brush/shower/dress

730 breakfast

745 drive

8-9 emails

9 venture A

930 checking facebook and perusing the

news 10 task B

1015 call with John 1030

undertaking B

11 talk with

associates 11:30

emails

12 lunch

1 calls/meeting

TIPS ON GETTING BETTER RESULTS FROM THE TIME TRACKING EXERCISE

1) You don't need to shut down at regular intervals. For instance, assuming you're composing a book or chipping away at an extraordinary venture, try not to record every brief time piece until you're finished with that task. There's no compelling reason to interfere with yourself in a significant undertaking just to record the time at regular intervals. At the point when you're finished chipping away at an assignment or action, that is an ideal opportunity to record how lengthy you spent on it.

2) You don't need to be awesome. Assuming that you endured 10 minutes cleaning your teeth and 5 minutes dressing, simply express "teeth/garments." Don't stress over planning the little things. That isn't what's going on with this activity. Cleaning your teeth sixty seconds quicker presumably won't change your life without a doubt. This activity is tied in with observing the significant propensities that are taking your time and denying you of the achievement you need. A portion of these destructive propensities you may be absolutely ignorant about, and this activity will assist you with recognizing those oblivious propensities right away and dispose of your significant visually impaired spots.

3) You needn't bother with a clock. Realizing that you burned through 33 minutes and 14 seconds on Facebook isn't any preferred or more accommodating over recording 30 minutes or 45 minutes. In any case, it's sufficiently nearby. Relinquish the should be a stickler during the Time Tracking Exercise. Significant propensities will end up being unmistakable,

whether or not you track in 15-moment or 15-second additions. Furthermore it takes significantly less work and time to follow 15-minute increments.

As Jim Rohn said, "what's not important to do is fundamental not to do." If you don't require more exact estimations, try not to invest in some opportunity to make more exact estimations. Following your time in 15-minute augmentations is sufficiently exact to allow you to see your significant vulnerable sides without investing in some opportunity to measure.

4) This ought not require some investment. Whenever I initially found out about this activity from Jim Rohn, I figured it would really sit around idly, not save personal time. I was so off-base! This activity requires some investment to do when you track your time in 15-minute augmentations, and I observed it promptly assisted me with acknowledging where I was investing an excessive amount of energy in ineffective exercises. This activity assisted me with recognizing my negative behavior patterns that were keeping me stuck, and it can do likewise for you. It additionally gives an incredible mental reminder that can hold you back from squandering a lot of energy on a useless propensity or activity.

For instance, assuming you need to record how long you've spent staring at the TV like clockwork, it sets out a great deal of open doors to switch off the TV and go accomplish something different all things considered. At regular intervals, you're making a mindfulness designated spot. During these designated spots, you'll have a choice: either keep doing what you're doing or pause and accomplish something else.
Having these designated spots can transform a 5-hour TV-watching gorge into 30 minutes of TV and four-and-a-half hours of a seriously satisfying movement that assists you with accomplishing your own objectives. We as a whole commit errors, and invest an excess of energy on useless undertakings. Having mindfulness designated spots helps you self-right and accomplish your objectives faster.

If you remain quiet about saying, "I ought to invest more energy on this" or "I should quit doing that," you'll observe that having these mindfulness designated spots makes a construction that assists you with taking your own recommendation and gain more headway quicker, without additional battle, stress or shame.

5) Keep doing this activity when you need better outcomes in your day to day existence. On the off chance that you wind up stuck and not gaining ground, return to this activity since it can help you quickly pinpoint where you're stalling out by recognizing propensities that are keeping you down.

This isn't simply an activity you do once and neglect. The more you utilize the Time Tracking Exercise, the more advantages you'll see.

6) Focus on your very own objectives and dreams, not society or others' thought process is ideal. It's critical to ensure you're pursuing your own objectives and dreams throughout everyday life. As you go through the Time Tracking Exercise

and make more mindfulness and change, simply ensure you're doing it for your own reasons. For instance, assuming you attempt to change yourself to bring in more cash since you believe that is what another person would need for you, you might wind up accomplishing an objective that is not even yours! Ensure you're focusing on your very own objectives and chipping away at what's generally significant for you. This activity is strong and it will work, so ensure it attempts to get what you truly need throughout everyday life, not what you figure others could need for you.

UNDERSTANDING YOUR RESULTS

I'll be straightforward with you. I didn't do the whole seven day stretch of this activity the initial time. Not even close.

It just took me three days to acknowledge I had a few truly negative behavior patterns that were denying me of my usefulness and keeping me stuck.

Here are a portion of the things I saw immediately:

I was investing an excess of energy in Facebook.

I was investing a lot of time checking emails.

I was not investing sufficient time really chipping away at my business and individual goals.

Before I began the Time Tracking Exercise, assuming somebody asked me how long seven days I functioned, I would have said 40-60. After the activity, I understood that, of those 40-60 hours I thought I was working, 25-30 of them were very useless exercises like riding the web, really taking a look at Facebook, irrelevant messages, sitting in front of the TV, and playing video games.

And out of the real time I spent dealing with the business, I viewed as its vast majority was spent on occupied, routine assignments that I might have employed a colleague to do while I zeroed in on the most noteworthy result exercises that would have a lot bigger impact on my pay and individual satisfaction. The more you see how you really invest your energy, the simpler it will be to roll out the right improvements for you.

It's not difficult to let somebody that know if they need to bring in more cash, they should work harder, or work more. But when you have a more accurate picture of how you're spending your time, you can start to focus on the small changes that make a BIG difference. That is the sort of influence that makes advancement success.

THE PROOF IS IN THE RESULTS

If you're as yet wary with regards to whether this little exercise merits doing, let me let you know that it totally is! The verification is in the results.

I seen prompt enhancements in my efficiency and pay as an entrepreneur in the wake of executing the illustrations I mastered utilizing this basic exercise.

It made my unsupportive, inefficient, and negative behavior patterns embarrassingly self-evident, and gave me a basic, direct, non-geek approach to rapidly dissect precisely the way in which I was investing my energy. Doing this basic time following activity resembles making an effort of unadulterated truth, and will give you quick input on what's not working for yourself and where you can make the most useful changes in your life.

Imagine your greatest objective or dream at the present time. Then imagine a role model or someone who has already achieved what you're looking to achieve, or at least something very similar to it. Then, envision going through a whole day with that individual and getting tweaked exhortation from them. What amount could you pay to get that sort of exhortation? Fortunately you don't need to pay for it. You can offer yourself the most ideal guidance utilizing the Time Tracking Exercise. What you really want to change to get what you need and accomplish your objectives will end up being unmistakable that you won't require a mentor or a coach to listen for a minute to do straightaway. You'll know what the following stage is for you, and it won't cost you a dime.

You can utilize this activity whenever you're prepared to gain ground and move to a more significant level of progress. Are mentors and coaches important and valuable? Absolutely! But don't think for a second that you need to find the perfect guru or mentor to show you how to achieve your goals and dreams. You can begin to gain ground and make advancement progress right now where you are with your own mindfulness and individual knowledge.

Every time I've shared this Time Tracking Exercise with instructing clients, they've encountered enormous leap forwards in private usefulness and viability. The framework works. The main inquiry is: will you work the system?

Without really having this data and knowing precisely the way that you're investing your energy, your greatest open doors for development will stay in your vulnerable side and evade you. You can peruse more books, purchase more

classes, review from more masters, enlist more mentors, and search out more tutors, yet until you at long last beginning taking your own recommendation, you'll miss the mark regarding your full potential.

As Arthur Ashe said, "Begin where you are. Use what you have. Give your best." You have undiscovered possibility inside you. You should simply take advantage of it, and this activity will permit you to do that.

Just attempt it. The most exceedingly terrible thing that could happen is that nothing changes. On the off chance that you employ a mentor for $5,000 and nothing occurs, you're out $5,000. Assuming that you do the Time Tracking Exercise and nothing occurs, you haven't lost anything. You should go for it and everything to gain.

I guarantee you this I've viewed as the quickest, most straightforward and easiest method for distinguishing any old propensities that are holding you back from accomplishing your objectives and dreams.

Once you've finished the Time Tracking Exercise, it's chance to continue on to the following stage and recognize your major habits.

STEP 2. DISTINGUISHING YOUR HABITS

Immediately in the wake of finishing your time following activity, begin recognizing all your major and minor propensities for how you spend your time.

The objective here is to make an expert rundown of your present propensities and exercises. *All that you recorded during the time following activity goes on this expert rundown of propensities right away, regardless of how little or how big.*

If you endured 15 minutes checking Twitter, that goes on your rundown. It doesn't make any difference how little or large the propensity is. For set it on your rundown to start.

When you're finished recognizing every one of your propensities and adding them to your lord list, begin to take it in. This is the manner by which you're as of now investing your energy. Does it look the manner in which you figured it could? A great many people concoct 20 to 50 propensities on their first rundown. Somewhat more or somewhat less is simply fine.

Remember, we were just estimating our time in brief additions such countless easily overlooked details like tying your shoes presumably didn't make it on the time following activity at any rate, and that is okay. A few things are excessively little and unimportant, and you might need to leave such propensities off the rundown. Dislike you will unexpectedly quit tying your shoes since you're investing an excess of energy in it. Be that as it may, assuming you went through 15 minutes or more in a solitary day on something, it's likely adequately significant to be on the expert rundown, basically for now.

DON'T LET PERFECTIONISM STOP YOU

Don't attempt to be great or "get it spot on" when you do these activities. This isn't a challenge or contest, and you're a victor here whether you do a smidgen or a ton. *Also I'm not saying that to be cheesy or excessively hopeful and encouraging.*

What I mean is that there's no "great" method for doing this. Regardless of whether you do the time following activity for 8 hours or two months, following this cycle will deliver new experiences, changes and results for you. Ensured. Investing more energy in it will regularly assist you with settling the score more outcomes, however don't let that prevent you from obtain the outcomes you can get assuming you just have a tad of time to put resources into doing this at the present time. *Every single propensity change counts.* Every single change can have an immense effect over the long haul. This guideline of how little changes make enormous contrasts additional time is known as the Snowball Effect,

and we'll cover it in more detail next.

Right presently, simply understand that you don't need to be wonderful when you do this. Following the interaction works. Also the more you follow it, the more it will work for you.

UNDERSTANDING THE SNOWBALL EFFECT

Most individuals drastically underrate the force of little changes to make colossal outcomes after some time. In the past model, we involved three hours every day of sitting in front of the TV as an example propensity to change. But many of us may not spend that much time on any one habit. We might have a few a lot more modest propensities that are keeping us stuck. That is totally fine. Even one small habit change of 15 minutes a day can make profoundly impactful changes over one year, five years, 10 years and more. An additional a 15 minutes of work a day is identical to in excess of seven eight-hour long periods of work consistently. Envision the amount more you could achieve with an additional multi week and a portion of work every year. Over fourty years, that is in excess of a whole year of additional work. Envision the amount more you could achieve with an additional a time of work. And all it would require to make that additional time is essentially dispense with a little 15-minute propensity like staring at the TV or surfing the web.

You can do significantly more in a short time a day than you could anticipate. Try not to allow little propensities to swindle you out of large success.

Little propensities snowball in manners that you couldn't envision at the present time. This is the manner by which certain individuals who begin working at the lowest pay permitted by law can significantly expand their pay over the long haul. Little, predictable changes in the end lead to colossal outcomes over time.

Never underrate the force of addressing a propensity, even a little one.

Step 3. Analyzing and Forecasting Your Current Habits

After you've made mindfulness in Step 1 and distinguished your lord rundown of propensities in Step 2, it's chance to dissect and comprehend your outcomes so you can see precisely the thing you've been doing, *how you've been getting it done*, *why you've been doing it*, and where those exercises will take you in the future.

ANALYZING

After the Time Tracking Exercise, we talked about why it's so essential to audit your outcomes and see which propensities you need to change. The present moment, we will take this individual audit of your propensities even further.

It's opportunity to dissect every one of your propensities and get a perfectly clear image of both the experts and the cons of each habit.

Whenever you have a propensity, you have that propensity in light of the fact that, eventually in your life, that propensity served you and gave a truly important and unmistakable result and advantage for you. Attempting to work on a propensity without understanding this can frequently basically prompt a perpetual pattern of enslavement, melancholy, and self-hatred since you figure you shouldn't accomplish something, yet you wind up doing it over, and over once more. The explanation you continue accomplishing something is on the grounds that it gives an advantage or result to you somehow or another, *and that result satisfies a fundamental requirement for you.* Understanding this is an essential advance to rolling out enduring improvement and staying away from the perpetual pattern of dependence and self-hatred that many succumb to.

With your time following outcomes before you, answer these inquiries concerning each major habit:

How could this propensity serve me? What advantages or rewards do I get by keeping up with this habit?

How could this propensity hurt me? What expenses or drawbacks do I need to look by keeping up with this habit?

How does this propensity help or backing others in my life?

How causes this propensity damage or challenge others in my

life?

Again, at whatever point you have a propensity, you have that propensity on the grounds that, eventually in your life, that propensity served you and gave an entirely significant and unmistakable result and advantage for you.

The accompanying inquiries and activities will assist you with plainly seeing both the settlements and advantages of every one of your propensities as well as the expenses. This data is unadulterated gold. *It's the most important data you might at any point get to work on your life, since self-information and mindfulness is the way in to all advance and power in life.*

Whenever you see just the expenses or just the settlements of a specific action, you will have an imbalanced viewpoint, and that imbalanced point of view will lead you to settle on poor long haul choices. For instance, assuming you see just the settlements of working extended periods of time, you might turn into a "obsessive worker" and penance other significant parts of your life to satisfy your imbalanced vision of your own life. This is the way certain individuals wind up working 10, 14, or 16 hours every day and totally obliterating their everyday life, public activity, and significant connections. *An imbalanced point of view on life prompts imbalanced movement, and that imbalanced action can prompt extremely adverse outcomes over time.*

For instance, drinking water is really great for you. Until you drink excessively and get water harming (which can be deadly). An overdose of something that is otherwise good can end up being an awful thing.

On the other hand, at whatever point you see just the expenses and drawbacks of a propensity, you will pummel yourself and stall out in pessimistic self talk and gloomy feelings each time you take part in that propensity, *despite the fact that that propensity is satisfying a reason in your life and giving you a substantial advantage (which you are not as of now seeing and acknowledging).*

According to John DeMartini, at whatever point you just see the adjustments and advantages of something throughout everyday life, you will become captivated by it and worshiped it. At the point when you see just the expenses and disadvantages of something throughout everyday life, you will become discouraged and put it underneath you. Both of these imbalanced viewpoints make pressure and adverse outcomes in your day to day existence, and the way to making better outcomes is to begin by making a more adjusted perspective.

ANALYZING YOUR HABITS AND ACHIEVING A BALANCED

UNDERSTANDING PERSPECTIVE

With your rundown of expert propensities before you, answer the accompanying inquiries and record any vital experiences and leap forwards you have along the way:

What might you say are your most useful and significant ways you've been spending your time?

What are your most un-useful and immaterial ways you've been spending your time?

What propensities do you promptly need to change?

What propensities are satisfactory for you at the present time (you see them as neither exceptionally certain nor very negative)?

What propensities do you love at the present time and need to keep?

Note: It's essential to have balance while dissecting and assessing yourself thusly. You could genuinely regret how you've been investing your energy, or you could feel glad for how well you're doing. In any case, it's essential to have balance. Truly, we as a whole do "great" things and "terrible" things (I utilize great and awful here as our very own, emotional internal considerations and decisions of our own conduct). That is simply aspect of being human.

So ensure you make note of somewhere around three beneficial routines and three negative behavior patterns to keep things in context assuming you're feeling excessively hopeful or excessively discouraged regarding your rundown. In any case, in the event that you just glance at your unfortunate behavior patterns, you'll have a discouraged and negative outlook on yourself. Assuming you just gander at your positive routines, you'll feel careless and proud.

Either way, you will be out of equilibrium, and assuming you keep up with that imbalanced viewpoint, you can wind up additional behaving destructively yourself and stalling out in blame.

Balance is the middle way that will take you where you need to go throughout everyday life. Continuously attempt to keep a reasonable perspective.

FORECASTING YOUR HABITS

Forecasting your propensities is one of the most remarkable 5-minute mental activities you can involve to make moment inspiration for change. This process
makes moment enthusiastic movements that will liberate you from old, unsupportive propensities, as well as help you recognize and like the positive routines you as of now have.

Forecasting can assist you with seeing the genuine expenses and advantages of each propensity in an amazing, overstated way. This can make it significantly simpler to see the genuine expenses and advantages (particularly ones you might have up until recently never recognized or appreciated).

Here's how.

Let's take "investing an excessive amount of energy staring at the TV" as an example propensity, and we should expect you estimated yourself going through three hours every day on this habit.

Now, to you envision yourself sitting in front of the TV for three hours per day today, tomorrow, the following day, and without fail for the remainder of your life. Would you be able to perceive how investing that much energy in this action consistently for the remainder of your life could impact both of you years, a decade, a long time from now?

Forecasting is essentially taking your present encounters and extending them into the future and attempting to comprehend what that future could be like.

Here are a few inquiries to help.

FORECASTING QUESTIONS

How much time will you consume in your time on earth on this propensity given your present every day time spent on it? Include that large number of hours, and perceive the amount of your life you're willing to put resources into that action. Three hours daily staring at the TV doesn't sound so awful, however when you add it up over fourty years, that is identical five straight long stretches of sitting in front of the TV 24/7!

How would you think spending X hours daily [doing your habit] will impact both of you years from now? A long time from now? A decade from now? A long time from now? A long time from now?

What else would you be able to do with X hours a day?

What would you be able to accomplish assuming you invested that energy in your most elevated need and most significant exercises instead?

Can you evaluate these outcomes some way or another? For instance, assuming you know you earn
$50 60 minutes, how much cash would that be assuming that you worked an additional a three hours per day as opposed to staring at the TV for three hours every day over the course of the following 10 years?

That would be:

$50 an hour x 3 hours per day x 260 work days a year x 10 years

= $390,000

Therefore, you can ascertain that your present propensity for sitting in front of the TV three hours daily will cost you $390,000 throughout the following decade, accepting you make no improvement in your capacity to acquire pay from working. North of 26 years, that is more than $1 million!

What assuming you spent each waking second on this propensity? What might your life look like?

I've found this is a powerful mental exercise that can create immediate shifts in your perceptions and beliefs. What if you spent every single waking moment on this habit? What if you spent 16 hours a day watching TV, seven days a week, 365 days a year? What would your life be like? What if you spent 16 hours a day working? What if you spent 16 hours a day doing nothing but checking Facebook?

I realize this likely sounds outrageous. Nobody could really do that, correct? Right. But that's not the point. The fact of the matter is that simply requiring one moment to envision what your daily routine would resemble assuming you experienced just that one propensity is a strong method for seeing both the upsides and downsides of your habits.

This activity can assist you with quickly placing things into an equilibrium viewpoint. For instance, you can compute how much cash you would make assuming you worked 16 hours every day, 7 days per week, 365 days per year. You can picture that much cash and see what it might be want to have that much money. You can likewise obviously see the downsides of that sort of way of life. No family, no companions, no public activity, no tomfoolery, no side interests... It would be a hopeless life, wouldn't it?

"Cash isn't all that matters" is a typical platitude. But the truth is *nothing* is everything. Love isn't all that matters, nor is wellbeing. Are this things important and good? Absolutely! But they're not everything. We as a whole need an equilibrium of various exercises, connections, propensities and encounters throughout everyday life. Zeroing in a lot on just a single part of life will constantly have unfortunate results, and this activity is intended to show them to you so you don't commit huge errors you'll later regret.

This activity can assist with placing things in context and permit you to see both the advantages and expenses of your current habits.

What assuming you at no point spent one more second on this propensity in the future for the remainder of your life?

This is taking the specific inverse perspective. What would your life be like if you just completely stopped watching TV and never turned a TV on again for the rest of your life? How would your life be different? Visualize this until you see both the rewards and costs of living such a lifestyle.

Do something similar for each propensity on your rundown like working, investing energy with family, key connections, side interests, etc.

Really invest time on this until you can see both the advantages and expenses of each propensity, the great ones and the terrible ones (as you would like to think). Begin to see the settlements of your vices, and the disadvantages of your beneficial routines that you might have never recognized before.

Who do you appreciate, or feel good feelings for who has this propensity or communicates a comparative habit?

This straightforward yet strong inquiry will assist you with seeing that you're in good company. There are many individuals whom you appreciate who express something similar or comparable propensities, and you can gain from this awareness.

Who do you abhorrence, or feel pessimistic feelings for who has this propensity or communicates a comparative habit?

Again, this is simply giving you significantly more consciousness of the equilibrium of life. You might observe yourself irate or annoyed with somebody whom you feel works excessively, for instance. But, just seeing this might assist you with finding in yourself your own novel articulation of working excessively or overexpressing a propensity at the expense of harming connections or other significant region of your life.

LIST OF FORECASTING QUESTIONS

How much time will you consume in your time on earth on this propensity given your present every day time spent on it?

How would you think spending X hours daily [doing your habit] will impact both of you years from now? A long time from now? A decade from now? A long time from now? A long time from now?

What else would you be able to do with X hours a day?

What would you be able to accomplish assuming you invested that energy in your most elevated need and most significant exercises instead?

Can you measure these outcomes somehow?

What assuming you spent each waking second on this propensity? What might your life look like?

What assuming you at no point spent one more second on this propensity in the future for the remainder of your life?

Who do you respect, or feel good feelings for who has this propensity or communicates a comparable habit?

Who do you abhorrence, or feel gloomy feelings for who has this propensity or communicates a comparative habit?

STEP 4. PRIORITIZING HABITS TO CHANGE

Now that you've dissected and guage your standard propensities exhaustively, you as of now have a much more clear image of what your propensities are and the impacts they're having on your life.

Many times, just recognizing, investigating and estimating your propensities will make a moment shift and assist you with taking out an unfortunate behavior pattern. Different times, you might have to take it much further prior to making genuine, enduring change.

This is the place where you will focus on your persistent vices all together with the goal that you can pick the main one to change first, and afterward go on from that point. On the off chance that you attempt to make progress with every one of your propensities without a moment's delay, it can really wind up causing more unevenness, stress, battle and disillusionment. An excess of progress can be negative and harmful, very much like drinking a lot of water.

Instead, simply center around addressing each significant propensity in turn until you've dominated it, and afterward continue on to the following one. It's definitely more critical to improve on one propensity for life than to make progress with a few propensities immediately and fall once more into your former ways presently after.

Focus is the way to working on propensities and making it last.

Presently that you've effectively estimated your propensities and examined them, record your rundown of negative behavior patterns indeed on another piece of paper. Now, inside thirty seconds, pick your #1 most significant propensity that you need to change right now.

Often, the primary propensity that rings a bell will be the one to begin with. The explanation you need to go through this activity as fast as conceivable is so you don't get stuck twofold speculating yourself and lose momentum.

As soon as you've picked the #1 propensity you will deal with evolving first, snatch another piece of paper and record the propensity at the top.

Next, return to your Time Tracking Sheet from Step 1, and record on your new clear piece of paper the entirety of the days and times you played out that habit.

Here's what it could look like:

HABIT TO CHANGE: WATCHING TV

Monday 5pm-7pm, 9:30pm-10:30pm
Tuesday 5:30pm-7pm, 9:30pm-
10:30pm Etc.

SCHEDULING YOUR HABIT CHANGE

Now that you have every one of your information in one spot from that one propensity, it's opportunity to plan your propensity change. Notice when and where you regularly play out that propensity. In the model above, notice that sitting in front of the TV appears to occur between 5pm-7pm and 9:30pm-10:30pm. These are the key times when you should know about your propensity and have one more strategy prepared of time with the goal that you don't rehash your old habits.

Here are the four key ways you can assist with ensuring propensity change at these key times:

SCHEDULE SOMETHING BETTER

Using this technique, you will plan something better and more best during your key propensity times. Utilizing the model from previously, between the long stretches of 5pm-7pm and 9:30pm-10:30pm, you would plan something better. For this situation, "better" signifies more charming, engaging or a good time for you actually. This should be something such a ton better that you could never imagine halting or stopping to take part in your old habit.

For instance, perhaps you plan an expert back rub between 5pm-7pm, and from 9:30pm-10:30pm, you plan a close date with your spouse.

The key here is to plan a movement that is a great deal more pleasant than the propensity that you will not consider it during those times.

SCHEDULE SOMETHING EXCLUSIVE

Using this strategy, you'll plan something that avoids the propensity from being plausible. For instance, assuming you golf from 5pm-7pm, you've avoided that propensity since you can't be staring at the TV and playing golf at the equivalent time.

An extraordinary method for planning something selective is to simply be elsewhere. Assuming you generally participate in a propensity in one area or spot (like at home), make arrangements to go out and be in an alternate place where it's simply impractical to proceed with that propensity during that time.

ELIMINATE TRIGGERS

Eliminating triggers implies killing signs or prompts that trigger your ongoing conduct. For instance, you could make a TV stand with an entryway that closes and close the entryway over the course of the day so that you're not as enticed to plunk down and watch TV.

Sometimes basically changing your course or timing can likewise assist with wiping out triggers. For instance, assuming you were attempting to stop espresso, and your typical course to work toward the beginning of the day goes by a Starbucks where you generally purchase espresso, you could basically take an alternate course to work that doesn't pass that area, along these lines staying away from the trigger altogether.

CHANGE THE ENVIRONMENT

Using this technique, you change the climate so it no longer backings the old propensity. For instance, you could drop your link membership or sell your TV. Albeit this might appear to be outrageous or incomprehensible in your circumstance, once in a while changing the climate can be the best method for ensuring long haul propensity change.

For instance, many medication addicts view that as in the event that they don't change their current circumstance, they can't resist the urge to fall once again into their old propensities for fixation. For genuine habit-forming conduct that you just apparently can't change differently, take a stab at changing the climate. This will frequently assist you with improving on the propensity for good.

WHAT ABOUT HABITS WITHOUT SET SCHEDULES?

If you need to address a propensity and notice that there is no set timetable for it, it might seem like these procedures won't work for you. The greater part of them will in any case turn out only great with a couple modifications.

The principal thing you need to do is figure out the thing may be setting off your propensity. In the model above, you could say that the hour of day was setting off the propensity for sitting in front of the TV. Numerous feelings, circumstances or occasions could set off a propensity. For instance, assuming you wind up pigging out on frozen yogurt and unhealthy food irregularly, dig further and see what may be setting off your behavior.

Oftentimes, it's an inclination or feeling inside that we will more often than not overlook, make light of or stow away from ourselves or others. A significant number of our negative behavior patterns are frequently unfortunate procedures for adapting to distressing circumstances and terrible emotions.

See assuming you can distinguish the specific feeling that will in general set off your persistent vice. Is it outrage, disappointment, misery, responsibility, disgrace, or something different? Simply

putting a name to the inclination can be an enormous advance forward in recognizing the hidden reasons for your habit.

Once you've distinguished the inclination, start to see when that feeling springs up. Are there certain circumstances or situations that tend to cause that emotion to occur? Many people find keeping a journal of their emotional states and reactions can help create more awareness and make change easier as well.

Without making this sort of mindfulness, it tends to be extremely difficult to address the propensity. You'll wind up having effectively eaten a whole container of frozen yogurt before you understand that you're feeling horrendous and committed an error. The key is to build your mindfulness so you notice the feelings prior and can stop the propensity sooner or keep it from happening altogether.

Make sure you recognize even little enhancements in propensity change. For instance, assuming you typically voraciously consume food a whole quart of frozen yogurt yet this time just eat 3/4ths of the compartment, that is progress! Any advancement ought to be recognized and celebrated. This supports your new propensity change and assists you with keeping that positive progress going.

When you notice a propensity being set off by an inclination, check whether you can track down a more certain, elective game-plan as opposed to gorging on unhealthy food.
Perhaps conversing with a friend or family member or compatriot about your feelings can assist with diffusing the pessimistic sentiments before the unfortunate behavior pattern dominates. Certain individuals observe that overwhelming activity can assist with diffusing these pessimistic feelings as well.

I would say with sincerely set off persistent vices, it's not so significant what you do when the inclination comes. *The important thing is that you do something different than just going through with your old habit.* Commonly being social and staying nearby others can help. Regularly, we attempt to stow away and stay away from these pessimistic feelings. Seldom individuals voraciously consume food with companions. More regularly, it's a single propensity. Just encircle yourself with companions can assist with diffusing the propensity since you can never again stow away it.

If you have a propensity and you don't know about what's setting off it or how to stop it, look to your feelings. Check whether you can distinguish the key, basic inclination that is answerable for setting off your propensity. Whenever you've done that, surface with one or a few methodologies for going in an alternate direction when that feeling comes up that will diffuse the propensity and make a new, more useful and satisfying propensity in its place.

STEP 5. IMPROVING EXISTING GOOD HABITS

Most individuals totally overlook this part of propensity change and usefulness. We think we want to zero in just on making progress with vices and not on working on our current propensities. However, ordinarily, the seeds for our most prominent victories are as of now filling in our momentum positive routines, and all we want is to water and sustain those seeds to permit them to bear significantly more fruit.

As a simple, easy to understand example, let's talk about money. If you already earn $10,000 a year from a habit (like writing, blogging, coaching, etc.), then you most likely have the potential to earn far more than that from that habit. The fact that you can already earn money from a current habit means that you have the potential to increase that amount of income by spending more time working, becoming a more productive worker, creating systems and processes to improve your results, leveraging other people's time, and other productivity strategies.

For instance, assuming you want to procure $20,000 and you as of now have a propensity that is acquiring you $10,000, you can perceive how straightforward it is produce those outcomes. Basically twofold your time, or twofold your usefulness, or a blend of both. Obviously, that is more difficult than one might expect. But, it should be really clear that doubling your results from a habit isn't an impossible task in such a situation.

It can be a little bit harder to see how to go from $10,000 to $100,000 or more, though. What's more that is the place where the compounding phenomenon we examined before becomes an integral factor. It most likely won't be quickly evident the way in which you can go from $10,000 to $100,000 or even $1,000,000 with that propensity. Truth be told, it could appear to be tremendously inconceivable. That is okay!

It's totally ordinary to feel as such, and you're perfectly located. It is feasible to further develop your outcomes 10x or more. The arrangement is to begin with little changes, keep on estimating your outcomes, and make slow changes and upgrades along the way.

The Japanese call this course of consistent improvement Kaizen. Furthermore that is the means by which extraordinary things are accomplished throughout everyday life. Reliably rolling out little improvements and upgrades prompts colossal changes in outcomes after some time. This is the compounding phenomenon we examined earlier.

Now, let me get straight to the point. I'm NOT saying that it will be simple, effortless

and that you're ensured to build your pay 10x or more assuming you do this.

This isn't about simple, moment, make easy money contrivances. This is tied in with rolling out little improvements that, after some time, can prompt colossal outcomes. *Indeed, making reliable, little changes after some time is regularly the best way to make a tremendous expansion in results.*

But regardless of whether you see a 10x expansion in pay, could everything will work out if you would make a few little changes and enhancements and go from
$10,000 to $11,000? Could an additional a $1,000 be important to you? Would it give sufficient inspiration and motivation to motivate you to make much more sure changes in your life?

It can be marvelous to ponder bringing in 10x more cash or having a 10x better relationship with your family, yet regularly a little improvement will have an adequately large impact to have a genuine effect in your life. And those small wins can provide the results and motivation you need to make even more changes, and so the virtuous cycle of Kaizen, constant improvement and small wins, keeps going.

Kaizen and steady improvement don't simply apply to bringing in cash. It applies to each part of your life - funds, profession, connections, otherworldliness, feelings, and whatever else that is critical to you.

It's much more straightforward to gauge a 10x expansion in pay than a 10x expansion in your bliss or relationship with your folks, and that is the reason I use pay for instance. But realize that these same principles apply to every area of your life. Assuming you made only one extra 5-minute call seven days to a friend or family member or relative or close buddy, you'd most likely feel more satisfied in your connections. It doesn't need to require some investment to get an enormous profit from your interest in each part of your life. The key is to track down those high-sway exercises or propensities that have a major effect without requiring a major speculation of time.

FALL IN LOVE WITH THE PROCESS, NOT THE RESULTS

I need to caution you here with regards to a typical snare individuals fall into. The vast majority of us fall head over heels for the outcomes and wind up disregarding the cycle. We go gaga for the cash, or the better relationship, or anything objectives we have, and we will more often than not neglect and limit the propensities, exercises and endeavors that got us those great outcomes in the first place.

You've presumably seen this plainly shown in a portion of your connections in

the past. You get into another relationship, things are going extraordinary, and you get into a decent notch where everything feels awesome.

Then you begin to slip a tad, unwittingly. Perhaps you quit regarding the other individual as exceptional as you did right away. Perhaps you invest somewhat more energy with your companions or staring at the TV than with your accomplice. Perhaps you quit making a special effort to give them gifts or do kind things for them. And afterward, you figure out they're leaving you since it's "dislike it used to be."

That's what happens when you fall in love with the results (having a good relationship that's going well) and ignore or minimize the habits and activities that led to those results (going out of your way to do kind deeds and show your appreciation for your partner, etc.) When you minimize or ignore these crucial habits, you stop doing them as often or altogether, and you erode the very foundation of the results you have fallen in love with! It's classic example of self-sabotage, and it's a common trap we all fall into at some point in our life.

So how would you keep away from this snare? Everything revolves around following this interaction we're going through in this book (the action and propensities for making mindfulness, assessing and guaging your current habits.)

By being more mindful of your propensities, you'll begin to see when you slip once more into old propensities or begin to abandon your new, further developed propensities. Keep in mind the force of mindfulness! It very well may be the way to opening the achievement you've been looking for.

AVOIDING MAJOR PSYCHOLOGICAL BARRIERS TO LASTING HABIT CHANGE

Humans have two significant mental inclinations that can imperil your capacity to keep up with new propensities and forge ahead with your way to success.

First, we will generally become acclimated to things the manner in which they are. Assuming you increment your pay by 10x, for instance, concentrates on show that it generally doesn't make you 10x more joyful. Indeed, it for the most part doesn't make you more joyful by any means after a specific pay level. Certainly, just after you accomplish that gigantic expansion in pay, you'll feel incredible. But that feeling soon fades, and you go back to your normal level of happiness. Being 10x more extravagant simply becomes normal.

Scientists call this peculiarity the indulgent treadmill, and if you don't see how it functions, it can cause a ton of pointless torment and languishing. In the event that you don't comprehend this peculiarity of human brain science, you'll be under the deception that having more cash or accomplishing your objective will make you for all time more joyful. In actuality, accomplishing an objective quite often just delivers a brief time of expanded bliss. From that point onward, you become acclimated to things the manner in which they are, and you return to your old degree of bliss. On the off chance that you wind up thinking, "On the off chance that I could accomplish this objective, I'll have it made!" you realize you've fallen into this snare. Feeling that you'll be more joyful in what's to come is a deception. Actually, you'll be generally blissful during the excursion as you develop and learn.

The most ideal way I've found to stay away from the snare of the indulgent treadmill is to defined objectives and propensities for myself that are both remunerating in the long haul and the diminutive term.

People who center completely around transient joy and achievement will more often than not end up troubled and feel unfulfilled on the grounds that they haven't accomplished more with their life. It turns out that focusing on short-term happiness and emotions doesn't often lead to long-term success. That is the reason showing up at parties consistently may feel incredible and fun at that point, yet following quite a long while you'll start to understand that you're not gaining ground in other significant region of your life.

If you've at any point felt like you ought to be more effective than you are presently or that you have companions or partners who have "cruised you by" monetarily, profoundly, sincerely or in another everyday issue, that is presumably in light of the fact that you've been zeroing in a lot on momentary outcomes around there of your life. The way to long haul achievement is long haul center. Some of the time the lower paying position or opportunity is seriously remunerating long haul. Now and again severing a relationship that you feel has no drawn out potential feels horrendous right away, yet can make the space you really want to find a superior long haul partner.

On the other hand, individuals who center totally around long haul results will generally feel unfulfilled and despondent on the grounds that they spend their entire lives attempting to accomplish something that they either never fully accomplish, or, when they in all actuality do accomplish it following quite a while, the bliss blurs considerably more rapidly than they envisioned.

This frequently prompts laments. You've likely seen individuals who invested a large portion of their energy working, and years after the fact lament not investing additional time with their family or voyaging. On the off chance that you end up zeroing in a lot on long haul results, you should think about adjusting your drawn out center for certain transient objectives and satisfying experiences.

The key for me, by and by, has been to zero in on the two long haul and momentary objectives. Whenever I find some kind of harmony, I wind up moving towards my drawn out objectives while partaking in the excursion a ton more.

Oftentimes, an unfortunate behavior pattern is just a subliminal way for us to satisfy present moment or long haul needs that aren't being met. So take a gander at your present equilibrium of present moment and long haul objectives and see what needs you probably won't meet right now that your negative behavior pattern is filling in for.

WE NEED SOMETHING NEW

A second possible mental obstruction to making progress with propensities is that we desire new encounters. People have a requirement for encountering new things throughout everyday life. Whenever things are new, we will generally exaggerate them. At the point when things are presently not new, we will generally underestimate them. That is the reason such countless new items say "New!" right on the name or in the promoting. This need to encounter new things can make a difficult example that initially makes and afterward annihilates numerous connections, organizations, and projects.

Most pop brain research books say that you can make another propensity in 30 days or 60 days, or some comparable number. As far as I can tell, it simply doesn't work that way. Indeed, it as a rule requires a little while of discipline to make another propensity. But that doesn't mean you now have that habit for life and never have to think about it again. Ordinarily, I've wound up making another propensity and staying with it for a couple of months, and afterward, when that propensity no longer feels new, I end up slipping once more into old propensities again or tracking down one more propensity to supplant that new one I really buckled down creating.

I'm speculating you've presumably had a comparable encounter before in light of the fact that I've seen a similar example over and over in myself, with my understudies and instructing clients, and with companions and family.

A typical example might be that it requires a couple of months to make a propensity and begin to see a few promising outcomes that get you invigorated and keep you needing to proceed with the propensity. Then, maybe a few months later, you hit a plateau. Perhaps you began the propensity for going to the exercise center and working out to shed pounds. So you lose 10 or 15 pounds in the initial not many months, and afterward the following not many months nothing changes. Your weight is remaining the equivalent despite the fact that you're trying sincerely, if not harder than when you initially began. That is the point at which we will quite often get deterred. What is the point of working out so a lot in the event that you're not come by results any longer? Thus we quit.

But this is the specific sort of self destructive behavior that prevents a great many people from accomplishing truly significant objectives throughout everyday life. Whenever I feel like I've hit a level throughout everyday life, I attempt to zero in on my drawn out objectives and targets. You could tell yourself, *"I realize I'm actually taking a stab at the rec center consistently and I haven't lost any weight in half a month, however I will continue onward. I know that assuming I keep up this degree of action, I will have an incredible outlook on myself and in the end I'll get to my optimal weight. But even if that doesn't happen, I'll feel better knowing that I'm a person who consistently works out than someone who just gives up when things get hard."*

Again, the key here is mindfulness. On the off chance that you wind up truly inspired with regards to another propensity, and unexpectedly become unmotivated, check in with your feelings again and see what's happening. Assuming you've as of now put in a couple of months making another propensity, it would be a disgrace to abandon it now. Whenever you hit a level, return in with your feelings and your objectives and commit once again to your habit.

This is another motivation behind why returning to the Time Tracking Exercise can be so useful. Commonly, we self destructive behavior unwittingly and don't see it. But the Time Tracking Exercise never lies. At the point when you measure how long you're turning out at the rec center or spending dealing with a significant task, you'll know right away on the off chance that you're meeting your objectives or not.

This is simply one more motivation behind why I suggest utilizing the Time Tracking Exercise at regular intervals or thereabouts. Normally, that is about when another propensity begins to lose steam and we begin searching out a new thing to have its spot. What's more that is the reason it's the ideal chance to return in, make more mindfulness, and ensure you're as yet on the right track.

STEP 6. CREATING MASSIVE RESULTS BY CHANGING ONE HABIT

I would say, the quickest method for obtain the best outcomes with improving on propensities is to zero in on your most significant propensity first. That is the reason we invested such a lot of energy prior distinguishing, focusing on, examining and anticipating habits.

Let's simply accept that it really requires 60 days to make another propensity. Furthermore we should expect that around 60 days after the fact, you'll begin to lose concentration Also let that propensity slip except if you make more mindfulness and continue to manage any levels or obstructions you face. And, we should accept that you're human, so you'll most likely spend an additional 60 days not chipping away at your propensities at all in light of the fact that startling things simply will generally occur throughout everyday life. At the point when you add all that up, what you see is that it truly takes the normal individual with regards to a large portion of a year to make a new, long lasting propensity. Perhaps you're way better than expected, and perhaps you're sub optimal, yet we should simply go with that figure for right now.

If this is valid, that implies you just truly have space in your life to make two new major long lasting propensities a year. What's more I have barely any familiarity with you, however actually I'm not truly adept at arranging things out any more than a year from now.

Heck, in any event, arranging out a day by day propensity plan a half year from now seems like an excessive lot of work for me.

For me, what it truly comes down to is that I've just got space for making and supporting one new propensity in the following not many months. That is my concentration - making one new propensity and adhering to it for the following 3-6 months.

I think certain individuals will quite often overdo it with propensity change. We attempt to change our eating routine, our exercise plan, our plan for getting work done, our rest plans, our dating life, our relationship with our family, our otherworldliness, and our own cleanliness at the same time. Let's just get real for a moment, all that sounds overpowering to me! Also it's not exceptionally commonsense, all things considered. Assuming you're similar to the vast majority, you've likely just got space for one new propensity right now.

So in the event that you've just truly got space for one new propensity at the present time, which one would it be advisable for it be?

You should zero in on your most significant propensity first and foremost.

If bringing in more cash is your greatest need at this moment, center around making another propensity that will assist you with doing that. If having a superior relationship with your family is the main need for you at this moment, make another propensity that will assist you with doing that. Assuming expanding your otherworldly information is your greatest need at this moment, center around making another propensity that will assist you with doing that. The key here is focus!

It's a piece cheesy, however I think the abbreviation for FOCUS (Follow One Course Until Successful) is an incredible method for recollecting the significance of zeroing in on making one new propensity. Try not to fall into the snare of attempting to change everything simultaneously, in light of the fact that it as a rule doesn't work, and it will in general end with more sensations of culpability, disgrace, outrage, and depression.

Instead, observe an everyday issue that is incredibly vital to you at this moment, and make another propensity that will assist you with feeling more satisfied and experience more achievement around there of your life.

It's truly only that simple.

And recollect the Snowball Effect we discussed before? It applies to propensity change, as well. Whenever you make another propensity that assists you with having a more effective profession, it will in general work on your connections, feelings, otherworldliness and different everyday issues. People are all encompassing. That implies that everything in our life influences all the other things. Whenever we work on one part of our life, it frequently works on different region of our life.

If you're behind on your bills, odds are good that you better get a wellbeing test notwithstanding a monetary exam. Why? Because if you haven't been paying attention to your finances, chances are you haven't been paying attention to your health either. While this standard works in the pessimistic for the vast majority, you can start to utilize it to your advantage.

When you make one new propensity that will assist you with satisfying your greatest need at the present time, it will consequently assist you with accomplishing more objectives in different everyday issues also. Why? Since as your mindfulness in one everyday issue develops, your attention to each everyday issue develops. Whenever you start to see all your awful monetary propensities and further develop them, you'll start to perceive how comparative feelings and persistent vices are harming your wellbeing and connections, as well. The greater part of what we do in life follows an example. *At the point when you find how to fix that awful monetary propensity you've fallen into, odds are you'll figure out how to fix those comparable persistent vices in your connections, wellbeing, feelings, otherworldliness, and other key region of your life.*

LESS IS MORE

With regards to making new propensities and undertakings, now and again toning it down would be best. It's smarter to zero in on improving on one significant propensity and prevailing than attempting to change everything simultaneously and falling flat. The more you center around improving on one propensity and making one new propensity, the simpler it will be to roll out that improvement stick. *That is the reason it's so essential to begin with your most significant propensity first.*

MORE TIPS FOR CREATING LASTING HABIT

CHANGE AND EMPOWERING HABITS

START EARLY

What do you do first thing when you awaken? In the event that you're similar to a great many people, you most likely follow the standard, worn out routine you've been accomplishing for quite a long time. It's become habitual.

The problem with unconsciously repeating old habits day in and day out is that they may no longer be supporting your current goals. Let's be honest: you're an alternate individual today than you were a decade prior, five years prior, or only one year prior. But being a different person with the same old habits won't get you where you want to go.

You must change a portion of those old propensities and ingrain new propensities that will assist you with accomplishing your objectives and dreams.

One of the best places to begin with regards to improving on propensities is in your initial morning schedule. What you do toward the beginning of the day establishes the rhythm for the remainder of the day.

If you feel like you simply lack opportunity and energy to begin another propensity at this moment, take a stab at setting your morning timer 30 minutes sooner and start your new propensity when you awaken. This can be an incredible method for beginning your new exercise propensity or make another propensity for contemplation or another significant movement that you can start without help from anyone else promptly in the morning.

SAYING NO

If your timetable is now full and you don't feel like you are investing sufficient energy in your greatest needs, that implies you have permitted low need undertakings to top off your schedule. Assuming that sounds natural, the best strategy is to begin saying no and dropping your responsibilities to undertakings that are done serving your best interests.

On some random week, you most likely get a few solicitations to invest your energy on exercises that aren't at the highest point of your needs list. That is fine. That is ordinary. Furthermore the best reaction you can make is to simply say no. Whenever you deny a low-need undertaking or responsibility, it makes space for you to approve of your most elevated priorities.

Note: We're discussing your needs here, not society's meaning of need for sure your folks think ought to be your needs. Assuming your most noteworthy need is chipping away at your business, for instance, and you turn down the potential chance to serve on a nearby cause pledge drive panel to invest more energy dealing with your business, that is a decent decision for you. Your foundation centered companions might believe you're childish, yet all the same that is just their viewpoint. Assuming your most noteworthy need and best utilization of time is developing your business, ultimately you'll have the option to give undeniably more to good cause in the long run.

If something is your main concern, it implies you want to safeguard your time and spotlight on it. Permitting low need assignments to gobble up your time doesn't serve you or any other person. Investing more energy in foundation might seem like the beneficial thing to do at that point, however over the long haul it's more terrible for yourself and everybody locally in the event that it's not your most elevated need movement. *On the off chance that you would be able, never penance a high need in your life to satisfy a low need need.*

When you're dealing with your most noteworthy need movement, odds are you will assist the vast majority the best you with canning. Yet, to do that, you should figure out how to deny anything that will get in your way.

If you approve of all that everybody requests that you do, you'll invest all your energy dealing with every other person's needs. But that's not the way to improve your life. The quickest method for further developing your life is to deal with your most elevated need. Dealing with something not exactly your most elevated need will motivate you less results.

WHAT TO DO ABOUT ADDICTIVE HABITS YOU CAN'T SEEM TO CHANGE

Disclaimer: I am not a clinical or mental master and can't offer you wellbeing or expert guidance. *Assuming you have a genuine dependence, I suggest seeing a clinical or mental expert to help you.*

What do you do in the event that you've attempted and attempted and just apparently can't get out from under an unfortunate behavior pattern that has been tormenting you for years?

Here, I'll share my own insight as a method for showing you what worked for myself and what could work for you to end even the most troublesome vices for good.

I used to be unbelievably dependent on playing computer games. Occasionally, I could in a real sense go through the whole day from awakening to nodding off playing computer games, with just little breaks in the middle to eat, drink and go to the washroom. It was most certainly not a sound propensity, and I attempted to stop out of the blue a few times with no achievement. A couple of days, weeks or months after the fact, I'd be once again at it playing computer games for quite a long time at a time. This propensity rehashed the same thing again and again, for quite some time, and it began to turn into a significant issue for me.

When I started to concentrate on brain research and self-awareness considerably more, I understood that this propensity existed on the grounds that it was satisfying a vital need and reason in my life.

When you have a vice you really can't break, ask yourself these questions:

How is this propensity helping me or supporting

me? What need or needs is this propensity

satisfying in my life?

If I quit doing this propensity totally, what might be absent from my life?

When I began to pose these inquiries, I understood that playing computer games was entertaining. Pretty obvious, right? But having fun is a very important aspect of life that most of us need and crave. Thus, I understood that to dispose of this propensity, I needed to supplant it with something fun.

After investing more energy becoming mindful and examining my propensity, I understood that it was likewise an incredible single action. As a loner, I can't invest an excessive amount of energy in friendly exercises or I wind up getting depleted and tired. So

at whatever point I attempted to simply go out additional with companions, it worked for a brief time, however at that point I would crash, need to invest some energy alone, and begin back at the computer game propensity again.

That's the way I understood that I expected to supplant this unfortunate behavior pattern with one more propensity that I could do without anyone else, not a social habit.

Finally, I understood that playing computer games was likewise a way for me to unwind. It would take my see any problems off ordinary concerns and stresses, and assist me with getting away into a really loosening up zone where I could simply zero in on playing and having fun.

In rundown, my habit-forming propensity for playing computer games helped add more enjoyable to my life, was a key lone movement I could return to when I wanted to be separated from everyone else, and was a way for me to unwind and unwind.

Can you presently start to see the reason why this propensity was so habit-forming for me? Whenever you have a propensity that satisfies numerous significant capacities or jobs in your day to day existence, *it will be difficult to fix except if you supplant it with different propensities that assist with satisfying those critical capacities and roles.*

With that as a main priority, I understood I expected to make one or a few new propensities that would help me 1) have a good time while 2) being separated from everyone else and 3) permit me to unwind, loosen up and de-stress.

Once I understood that, it was truly simple to discover a few elective propensities. Everything I did was lock myself in my room, turn of my cell and any interruptions, get a note pad and pen and began conceptualizing exercises I could do that would satisfy at least one of those needs.

Here are some examples:

Walking

Hiking

Running

Taking

naps

Once I had my rundown of thoughts, it turned into significantly more straightforward to make some new habits

and dispose of my propensity for playing computer games entirely.

There are a couple of key focal points that you ought to gain from my

model. Above all else, comprehend the fundamental necessities and jobs

your propensity fulfills.
Without this mindfulness, you'll become furious, irritated, discouraged, and frustrated
when you attempt to address your propensity and eventually fall flat. The explanation you continue to fizzle is on the grounds that your propensity gives significant advantages to your life that you really want to track down one more approach to replace.

Second, *don't attempt to supplant a propensity with a non-free propensity.* For instance, as a self observer, I couldn't just spend time with companions and go to more get-togethers to supplant my computer game propensity, since I really wanted a free propensity that I could do alone.

If you're an outgoing individual, and you end up getting dependent on smoking or drinking at get-togethers, you could begin contacting new groups of friends where individuals don't smoke or drink to help dispose of that habit. Remaining at home more most likely wouldn't be a decent answer for an outgoing person. To this end mindfulness is so significant, and is a definitive key to enduring propensity change.

Third, *troublesome propensities become simpler to change when you have numerous substitute propensities or practices to redress.* Assuming I just had climbing on my rundown of substitute propensities for playing computer games, I would be extremely restricted in my choices. On the off chance that I hyper-extended a lower leg, for instance, and couldn't go climbing, I would probably fall once more into the propensity for computer games rapidly in light of the fact that I wouldn't have the option to go climbing to satisfy my requirement for no particular reason and unwinding. *Try not to restrict yourself to just a couple of substitutes for an unfortunate behavior pattern. The more choices you have, the more probable your*

progressions of achievement in making enduring propensity change.
Assuming that you need to put an hour or more in conceptualizing thoughts
and getting innovative, it'll be perhaps the best venture of time you can
make.

CREATING ACCOUNTABILITY AND GETTING THE SUPPORT OF

OTHERS

Another incredible method for assisting with propensity change is to enroll
the help of others. AA has assisted great many individuals with stopping their
dependence on liquor by utilizing bunch backing, responsibility and
otherworldliness to assist individuals with recuperating passionate injuries,
settle on better choices and change old habits.

You don't need to experience the ill effects of a genuine dependence on
benefit from

responsibility and gathering support. Regardless of whether you need to begin
practicing more, eat a better eating regimen, or invest more energy chipping
away at another task, responsibility and gathering backing can be an
enormous inspiration and supportive resource for get your new propensity on
track.

Today with web-based media, discussions, online gatherings and locales like
MeetUp.com, it's simpler than at any other time to observe a gathering like
you who can assist with keeping you responsible and urge you to continue to
gain positive headway. Assuming you're feeling stuck, don't have the
foggiest idea what gathering to go to, and simply need some help and to
interface with other people who are additionally attempting to make good
changes in their lives, come join our free gathering on Facebook and how
about we help each other make a few better propensities. You can join us at
www.facebook.com/gatherings/EntrepreneurSuccessGroup

MODEL AND ASSOCIATE WITH SUCCESSFUL PEOPLE

Who do you spend time with and how would they influence you?

Individuals we invest energy with wind up making a progressive, however
consistent draw on us toward the path they're going. Assuming that you
spend time with individuals who drink a ton, odds are you'll drink more.
Assuming you spend time with individuals who go to the drama consistently,
odds are you'll invest more energy at the show. It sounds self-evident,

Getting a back rub or bodywork

Exploring another put or area of town on my

own Reading

Brainstorming novel thoughts, what should be done, marketable strategies and projects

however the greater part of us don't invest sufficient energy chipping away at developing connections that help us and assist us with moving in the right direction.

We likewise will quite often think about ourselves, intentionally and subliminally, to individuals we invest time with. Who do you contrast yourself with? Assuming you contrast yourself with inefficient individuals, you could feel like you're unquestionably useful and fruitful. But if you compare yourself to a super- productive multimillionaire, you might feel lazy and unproductive in comparison. It's all family member. Your companion gathering will decide, generally speaking, how you see yourself, who you intentionally and unwittingly contrast yourself with, and what progress you do or don't make as a result.

If you have need to begin a propensity for running a long distance race, for instance, and none of your companions might in fact run a mile, it will make that propensity considerably harder to frame. You'll most likely need to venture out and meet new individuals - different sprinters who you can prepare with, gain from, and consider you responsible to your goals.

When you're attempting to make changes in any aspect of your life, hope to see who you realize who is on a comparative way as of now and attempt to invest more energy with

them. If you don't know anyone who would be a good fit, then reach out and try to meet new people who are on the same path. Life's too short to even think about traveling solo or with some unacceptable companions.

If you need to go up and accomplish new and greater objectives, encircle yourself with other people who are doing likewise or who have effectively accomplished what you need to accomplish. It'll make your excursion significantly simpler, and much more tomfoolery and fulfilling.

Keep Making Progress

It's difficult to gain predictable headway in the correct bearing without mindfulness. Assuming that you're mindful, you won't allow persistent vices to loot your wellbeing, take your prosperity, and obliterate your most valuable connections. That is the reason we began this excursion with the Time Tracking Exercise since when you do it right, you can't deceive yourself any longer. The numbers don't lie. Whenever you begin to focus on how you're really investing your energy, you can't conceal your vices any longer. You can't conceal reality whenever you've seen it.

For those of you who are truly roused, you can utilize a similar six stage process in this book to work on pretty much every aspect of your life. Notwithstanding the Time Tracking Exercise, you can utilize a comparable exercise to follow other key parts of your life. You can follow your costs and what they're meaning for your funds. You can follow your eating routine and exercise propensities to decide what they're meaning for your wellbeing. You can follow your social communications to decide what they're meaning for your public activity and relationships.

Whenever you accomplish something that expands your mindfulness, you will start to work on your life. Assuming this book has assisted you with expanding your consciousness of how you invest your energy, then, at that point, I've done my job.

Now it's your chance to utilize that new attention to make another propensity and change your life forever.

Here's to your prosperity!